Patterns

Written by Francesca Motisi

Wayland

CRISS X CROSS

Boxes   Light
Changes Patterns
Holes   Textures
Journeys Wheels

Picture acknowledgements

The publishers would like to thank the following for allowing their photographs to be reproduced in this book: Cephas 12 (W. Geiersperger), 24 (Stuart Boreham); Bruce Coleman Ltd 4 (Peter Davey), 5 above (Mark N. Boulton), 7 (Dr Eckart Pott), 9 above (Kim Taylor) below (Norman Owen Tomalin), 10 (Prato), 18 left (David Goulston), above (L. C. Marigo), 26 below (Gerald Cubitt); Chris Fairclough *cover*, 6 above, 8, 11, 14, 15 above, 20, 26 above, 28 below, 29 (both); Himalayan Images 23 above; Oxford Scientific Films Ltd 6 below (Mark Hamblin), 13 (Harold Taylor), 21 below (Earth scenes/John Gerlach); Wayland Picture Library *title page*, 15 below, 19, 22, 28 above; ZEFA 5 below, 16, 17, 18 right, 25, 27.

First published in 1992 by
Wayland (Publishers) Ltd
61 Western Road, Hove
East Sussex BN3 1JD, England

© Copyright 1992 Wayland (Publishers) Ltd

Editor: Francesca Motisi
Designers: Jean and Robert Wheeler

Consultant: Alison Watkins is an experienced teacher with a special interest in language and reading. She has been a class teacher but at present is the special needs coordinator for a school in Hackney. Alison wrote the notes for parents and teachers and provided the topic web.

British Library Cataloguing in Publication Data

Motisi, Francesca
Patterns. – (Criss cross)
I. Title II. Series
516

ISBN 0-7502-0352-8

Typeset by DJS Fotoset Ltd, Brighton, Sussex

Printed and bound in Italy by L.E.G.O. S.p.A., Vicenza

Contents

The answers to the questions in the text can be found on page 32. Words that appear in **bold** in the text are explained in the glossary on page 32.

Patterns in nature

There are patterns in nature and patterns made by people.

These animals have patterns on their coats
for a reason.
Their spots and stripes help them to hide.
Why do they need to hide?

Birds

All birds' feathers have lovely patterns.

This duck's feathers stop it from getting cold and wet and help it to fly.

◀ This is a close-up view of a jay's wing.

Often male birds have brighter feathers than female birds. This helps the male bird to find a **mate**.

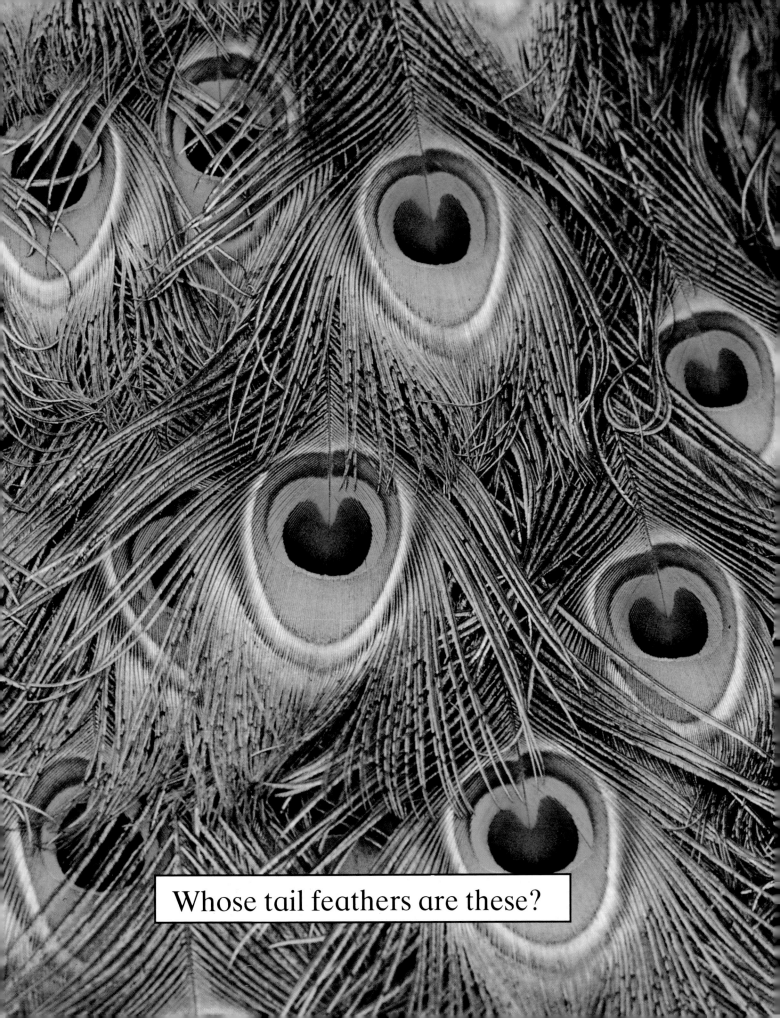

Whose tail feathers are these?

Butterflies

Butterflies have the same pattern on both wings. The pattern is **symmetrical**. Look at the picture on page 9. You will see a close-up view of this tortoiseshell butterfly's wing.

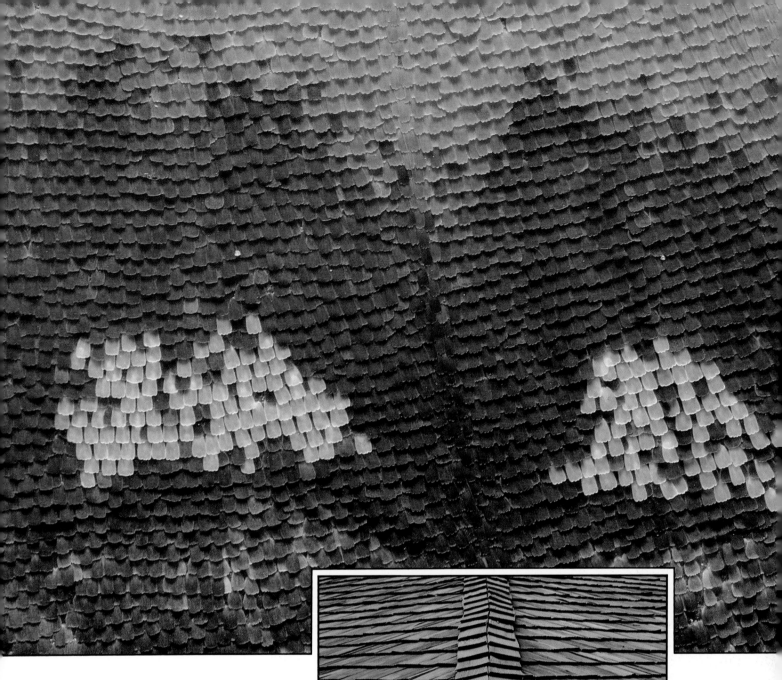

Each wing is
made from tiny
overlapping scales.

Compare it with the
pattern these roof
tiles make.

9

Bees build their **honeycomb** in a **hexagonal** pattern.

These
concrete pipes
make a pattern
like the bees'
honeycomb.

Leaves

Plants have patterns on their leaves. In the autumn you can collect fallen leaves and make leaf rubbings. You can do this by using a wax crayon and a piece of paper. Place the paper over a leaf and then rub gently with the crayon.

The veins on leaves make a pattern. You can make patterns by printing with fallen leaves.

These children are painting one side of the leaf and then gently pressing the leaf on to a piece of paper.

13

Trees and bark

When a tree trunk is cut you can see a **circular** pattern. You can find out the age of the tree by counting the rings.

Look at the patterns on a tree trunk. You could take a **bark** rubbing by using a wax crayon and a large piece of paper.

Patterns in the

Ploughed fields have a stripy pattern.
What made the stripes and why?

landscape

People or nature can change the pattern of the **landscape**. When the wind blows it changes the pattern in the sand.

Patterns made

People like patterns – on their carpets, on their dishes and on their clothes. Where else have you seen a pattern?

by people

Making lace takes a long time. Some lace patterns look like the patterns made by frost and snow.

This girl has a stripy pattern on her jumper and skirt. What else has a stripy pattern in this book?

Buildings

Find the patterns in this photograph.

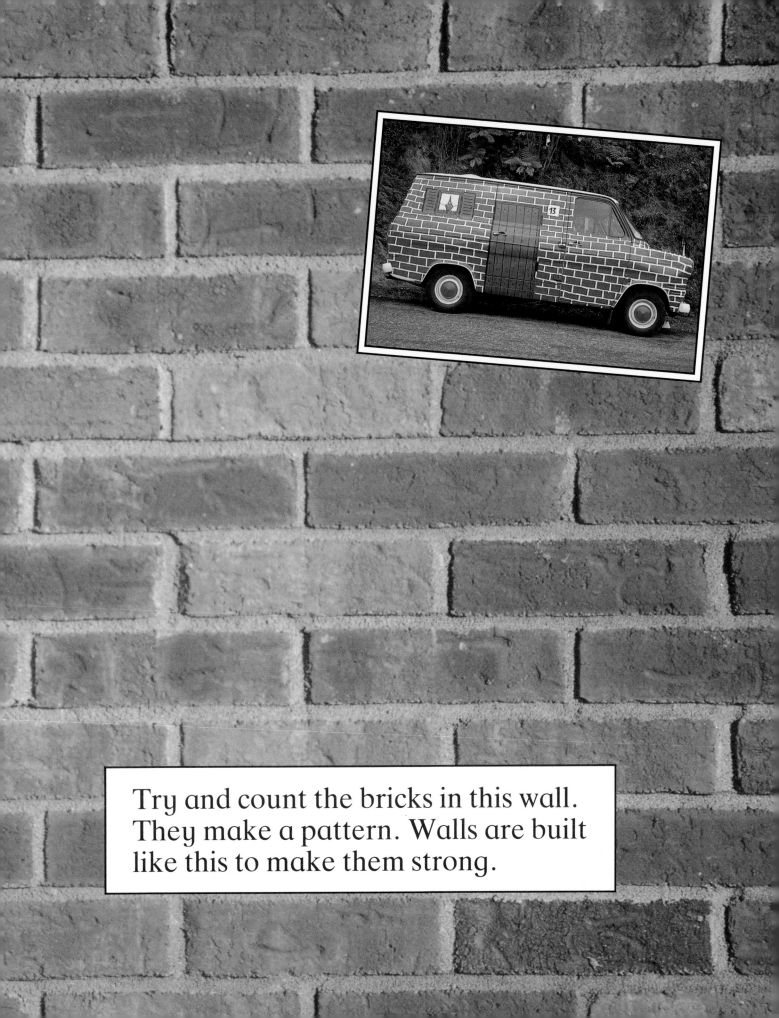

Try and count the bricks in this wall.
They make a pattern. Walls are built
like this to make them strong.

Most buildings have patterns on them.
Look at other buildings and see how many
patterns you can find.

The pattern on this roof will change when the **roofer** adds tiles. Look at page 9 to see the new pattern.

More patterns

When you walk in the sand you leave a pattern of footprints behind you! The marks you make are called tracks.

Animals and birds leave patterns in the mud or snow. These are also called tracks.

Whose tracks are these?
Look at the bottom of page 5 to find the owner. It must have big paws!

Look around your school, home and park. Find as many different patterns as you can.

As you will have seen from this book there are many sorts of patterns! They are not all easy to find.

Notes for parents and teachers

Maths
- An appreciation of pattern and sequence is fundamental to a lot of mathematical concepts.
- Children can investigate patterns in number using multilink cubes, number lines, beads, squared paper and number squares.
- Children can look for maths in the environment. Set up a maths pattern trail around the school and playground.

Language
- At this stage children are developing their understanding of the alphabet. Children can make patterns using letters and words.
- It is commonly accepted that reading rhymes and stories with meaningful repetition helps children learn to read. Children can look for patterns in stories and rhymes. They can write their own poem with a pattern.

Science and Technology
- There is huge potential for discovering patterns in the animal world. Using the wonderful photographs in this book can lead to discussions about camouflage, why birds' feathers make such a pattern, why male birds often have more colourful plumage than the females, etc.
- In order to find the appropriate pattern in nature and elsewhere it is necessary to trace a sequence through more than once e.g. the development of frogspawn-frog-frogspawn . . .
- Looking closely at insects and minibeasts can lead to interesting discoveries (patterns, symmetry, colour, shape, etc.) plus patterns in the trails they leave, how they move etc.

Geography
- Children can explore patterns in the seasons. Then within each season they can discover patterns caused by the elements e.g. sun, rain, wind, snow, fog, ice etc.
- Investigating their environment can lead to many discoveries e.g. pattern symmetry in buildings (count the number of windows, doors, chimneys, flats in a block etc.) Walls can be used as a basis for the children's own designs. Suitable subjects for 5-6 year-olds could be Humpty Dumpty and other nursery rhymes.

History
- Many opportunities will arise in which children can be helped to discover patterns in exploring historical concepts of time, change, past, present and future.

Multicultural
- Muslim women and girls decorate the back and palms of their hands with beautiful floral or abstract patterns called Mendhi.
- Also during the festival of Divali Rangoli patterns are made. Many other cultures e.g. Native Americans have strong designs and patterns (sand painting, basket designs, beadwork, Navajo blankets, patterned pots etc.)

P.E./Dance/Drama
- Mathematical concepts e.g. mirror symmetry can be developed through dance and P.E.

Music
- Look at musical notes, or signs on paper, and you can see a pattern. Children can write their own music notes or symbols.

Art/Craft
- Children can create random patterns (e.g. take a line for a walk, drop thinly mixed paint from a brush on to wet paper).
- Weaving using two coloured strips of sugar paper.
- Making patterns of stitches through sewing.
- Use rubber stamps to make borders or designs.
- Look closely at patterned fabrics. Recreate your own through printing with vegetables and fruits, or batik (a method of colouring and patterning fabric using wax resist and dyes).

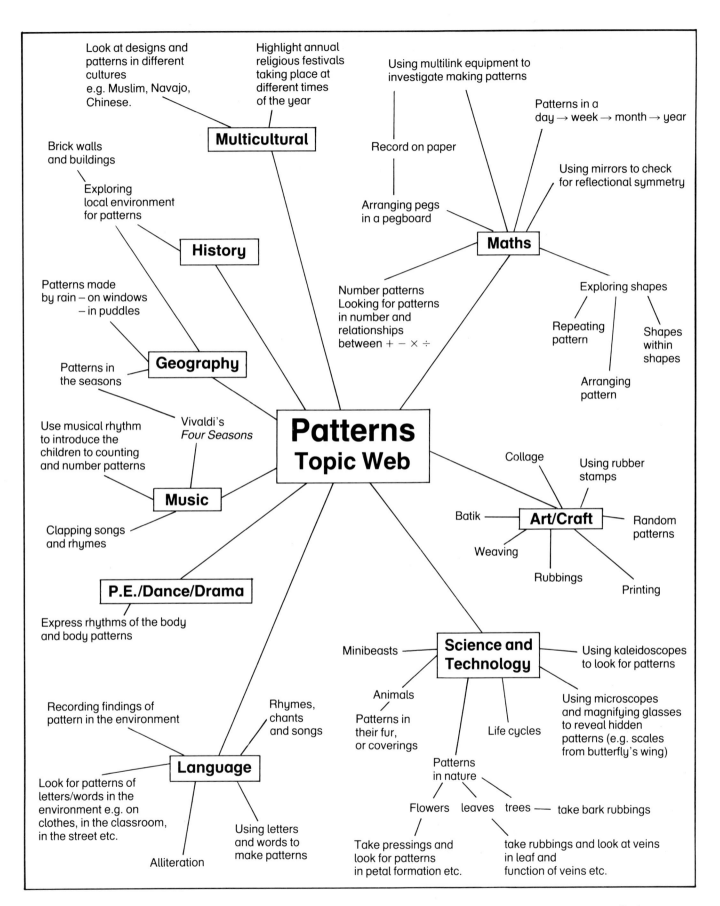

Look at designs and patterns in different cultures e.g. Muslim, Navajo, Chinese.

Highlight annual religious festivals taking place at different times of the year

Using multilink equipment to investigate making patterns

Patterns in a day → week → month → year

Record on paper

Using mirrors to check for reflectional symmetry

Multicultural

Brick walls and buildings

Exploring local environment for patterns

Arranging pegs in a pegboard

History

Maths

Patterns made by rain – on windows – in puddles

Number patterns Looking for patterns in number and relationships between + − × ÷

Exploring shapes

Geography

Repeating pattern

Shapes within shapes

Patterns in the seasons

Arranging pattern

Use musical rhythm to introduce the children to counting and number patterns

Vivaldi's *Four Seasons*

Patterns Topic Web

Collage

Using rubber stamps

Music

Batik

Art/Craft

Random patterns

Clapping songs and rhymes

Weaving

Rubbings

Printing

P.E./Dance/Drama

Express rhythms of the body and body patterns

Science and Technology

Using kaleidoscopes to look for patterns

Minibeasts

Animals

Using microscopes and magnifying glasses to reveal hidden patterns (e.g. scales from butterfly's wing)

Recording findings of pattern in the environment

Rhymes, chants and songs

Patterns in their fur, or coverings

Life cycles

Language

Look for patterns of letters/words in the environment e.g. on clothes, in the classroom, in the street etc.

Patterns in nature

Flowers   leaves   trees —— take bark rubbings

Using letters and words to make patterns

Alliteration

Take pressings and look for patterns in petal formation etc.

take rubbings and look at veins in leaf and function of veins etc.

31

Glossary

Bark   The outer layer of a tree trunk.

Circular   Something that is shaped like a circle.

Hexagonal   Something that has a shape with six sides.

Honeycomb   A honeycomb is made by bees from wax; honey is stored in its six-sided cells, eggs are laid and larvae develop.

Landscape   The view you can see all around you.

Mate   An animal or bird's partner.

Overlapping   Lying partly on top of something else, like tiles on a roof.

Roofer   Someone who builds roofs.

Symmetrical   A shape is symmetrical when both sides match up exactly.

Index

Answers

Page 5 Wild animals have patterns on their coats for camouflage so that they can blend in with their background. An animal which is hunted (the prey) is camouflaged to make it harder to find. A hunting animal (the predator) is camouflaged to hide it from its prey.

Page 7 A male peacock.

Page 16 A farmer made the stripes by using a tractor to plough the field, so that new crops could be planted.

Page 21 Other stripy patterns can be found on the zebras on page 4, on the tiger on page 5, and on the ploughed field on page 16.

Page 27 A tiger.